THE LIFE AND TIMES OF

JACKIE ONASSIS

Esme Hawes

CHELSEA HOUSE PUBLISHERS
Philadelphia

First published in traditional hardback edition
© 1998 by Chelsea House Publishers.
Printed in Hong Kong
Copyright © Parragon Book Service Ltd 1995
Unit 13–17, Avonbridge Trading Estate, Atlantic Road
Avonmouth, Bristol, England BS11 9QD

Illustrations courtesy of Hulton Deutsch Collection; London
Features International; Mirror Syndication International;
Peter Newark's American Pictures

Library of Congress Cataloging-in-Publication Data
Hawes, Esme.
    The life and times of Jackie Onassis / by Esme Hawes.
        p.   cm.
    Originally published: London: Parragon Books, 1996.
    Includes index.
    Summary: Biography of the wife of President John Kennedy
beginning with her childhood and including her years in
"Camelot," life with Aristotle Onassis, and later years as a
grandmother.
    ISBN 0-7910-4640-0 (hc)
    1. Onassis, Jacqueline Kennedy, 1929-1994 —Juvenile
literature.   2. Celebrities—United States—Biography—
Juvenile literature.   3. Presidents' spouses—United States—
Biography—Juvenile literature. [1. Onassis, Jacqueline
Kennedy, 1929-1994.   2. First ladies.   3. Women—Biography.]
I. Title.
CT275.0552H39 1997
973.922'092—dc21
    [B]   97-26941
                                                      CIP
                                                          AC

CONTENTS

Jackie at age 10

CHILDHOOD

In 1927, at the age of thirty-seven, Jack Bouvier was considered to be one of New York's most eligible bachelors. He was tall, dark, and handsome, and was commonly referred to as "Black Jack," both for his rugged good looks and his devilish reputation. The son of a lawyer (known as "The Major"), Jack was expelled from school for instigating poker games, but he eventually made it to Yale, where he wound up at the bottom of the class. After he had worked on Wall Street for a while, his wealthy family set him up in business. Although he did quite well, his expenditure far exceeded his income; the nightly revelries he held at his apartment on Park Avenue were the talk of the town. Family and friends looked on in dismay as Black Jack wreaked havoc with the reputations of their daughters.

It was traditional for top-society New York families to spend the hot summer months on Long Island and, naturally, the Bouviers did so too. The year 1927 was no exception. At their exclusive local social club, the Bouviers encountered the Lees, not as well established on the social ladder but considered a "respectable family," and James T. Lee was president of the New York Central Savings Bank. The Lees had three daughters; it is said of the middle one, Janet, that the moment she laid eyes on Bud Bouvier, Black Jack's brother, she fell madly in love. However, Bud was a divorced alcoholic and the relationship went nowhere, so instead she married his dashing brother, Jack. Jack had, apparently, been engaged many times before but there must have been something different about Janet, because on July 7, 1928, the couple did make it to the altar in East Hampton—an occasion the *East Hampton Star* declared to be the social event of the season, with hundreds of Wall Street types attending the wedding ceremony. The following morning the couple set off for their honeymoon in Europe aboard the *S.S. Aquitania*. That very first day Jack began flirting with a sixteen-year-old passenger and the pattern of their marriage was set.

On July 28, 1929, their first child, Jacqueline, was born. This event was closely followed by the death (from cirrhosis of the liver) of Bud Bouvier, who was to have been the baby's godfather. Bud's nine-year-old son, Miche, stood in for him. The recent Wall Street Crash had left Jack at the financial mercy of his father-in-law, and James Lee now agreed to lend him a rent-free apartment—but only if he gave up his flamboyant lifestyle. Jack didn't have any choice, and the family moved in to the vast apartment. Smarting from Lee's restrictions, Jack immediately began to refurbish the place, installing, among other things, a gym complete with sunlamps; he also hired a cook, two maids, and an English nanny. On March 3, 1933, the couple had a second daughter, Caroline Lee.

Jackie and Caroline

Jacqueline Kennedy

SCHOOL DAYS

At the exclusive Chapin School for Girls in Manhattan, little Jackie—intelligent and a precocious reader—would finish her lessons before any of the other pupils, but she was boisterous and unruly. Her prime interest was horses and even as a young girl she took part in gymkhanas (games on horseback). In the meantime Black Jack continued womanizing and losing money at gambling. "Why don't you go and exercise your pony?" became the usual signal to Jackie that her parents were about to have another fight and that she should leave the room. It was no secret, even to their small daughters, that the Bouviers' marriage was in trouble. Jack was often seen in the company of attractive young women, and Janet refused to be seen with him at all. Eventually, in June 1934, a photographer took a devastating photo in which Jack was clearly seen holding hands with another woman behind Janet's back. It appeared in various papers; Janet's father could take no more and urged her to see a divorce lawyer. At first she demurred, but on September 30, 1936, when Jackie was seven, Janet demanded a six-month trial separation, legally drawn up. Black Jack moved into the Westbury Hotel on Madison Avenue.

Jack would take the girls out every weekend and spoil them rotten. He was hugely extravagant, while Janet was soon seen as the severe mother and disciplinarian. Jackie, especially, became daddy's girl. The separation period came to an end and Jack returned to the family home, but things went from bad to worse and they split up again. By 1938 the mere mention of her husband's name would drive Janet into a state of fury, and the competition between their parents became perceptible in the faces of their children. Jackie, once bright and confident, now seemed aloof and isolated and, for the first time ever, she didn't make it to the top of her class, while Lee had uncontrollable crying fits.

By 1939 Janet was beyond caring what people thought. She hired a private detective and gave the evidence he collected to the press. On January 26, 1940, the New York *Daily Mirror* announced "Society Broker Sued for Divorce"; the story ran for days in every tabloid in the country. On June 6 Janet took the children to Reno, Nevada, to get a divorce on grounds of "extreme mental cruelty."

At the time of the divorce, Jacqueline was nearly eleven years old. Though her life remained basically unchanged, she became even more aloof, reading more than ever and devoting her entire spare time to horses. In 1941 she scored a double victory in a competition at Madison Square Garden.

Black Jack, divorced at fifty, began to date some of the youngest and most beautiful women in New York, and Janet encouraged her friends to introduce her to as many men as possible. Eventually she encountered Hugh Auchincloss, a lawyer of Scottish descent who had set up an investment banking firm and was rich, stable, and dull. He had already been divorced twice—his second wife, Nina Gore Vidal, was the mother of the famous writer. In June 1942, with the Second World War raging, Hugh, who had volunteered for the U.S. navy, was told to report immediately to Kingston, Jamaica. Janet rushed to Virginia with her two daughters to bid him good-bye, and the couple spontaneously decided to get married. Hugh already had three children of his own, and the service took place on his croquet lawn with all five offspring as the witnesses.

The Life and Times of

By September Hugh had been recalled from Jamaica and relocated to a desk job in Washington, D.C. Janet was relieved to have found a man she admired who could look after her two daughters financially, and the couple went on to have two more children of their own, Janet, Jr., and Jamie. Hugh was fabulously wealthy and extremely well connected. Janet took over his Virginia estate, Merrywood, and had the whole place redecorated, complete with Olympic-size swimming pool, indoor badminton court, and stables.

Initially Jackie wrote copious letters to her father, complaining about her impossibly boring stepfather, but after the family spent the summer of 1943 at Hugh's summer house—a huge estate called Hammersmith Farm on Cape Cod—she cheered up considerably. The house had twenty-eight rooms and a working farm. Jackie loved helping her new siblings with the farm animals, and she was personally responsible for feeding the hens each day. Her letters became much more optimistic while her father grew increasingly depressed. That Christmas the girls spent the season with the Auchinclosses in Virginia while their father drank himself silly in East Hampton. By Easter he had voluntarily committed himself to the same alcohol dependency unit that his brother had attended some sixteen years earlier.

In 1944 Jackie enrolled as a boarder at Miss Porter's School in Connecticut. She didn't have many friends and, though a good student academically, her main concerns were financial since she had no money and all the other girls at Porter's had a great deal. She grew astute at playing her parents off against each other in order to get money. Her greatest pleasure was having her father visit—which was also the greatest pleasure of most of the other girls, much to Jackie's chagrin. She got straight As in all her classes, but to her fellow pupils she seemed distant and slightly standoffish, never confiding her secrets to the other girls. When she graduated from high school in June 1947, she wrote in her class yearbook that her ambition in life was "not to be a housewife."

Both her parents considered this to be a stab at her mother.

Later that summer Jackie had a formal coming out party at Hammersmith Farm to which she personally invited three hundred guests. She was named "Deb of the Year" and appeared in a number of magazines and gossip columns. In the autumn she started at Vassar, a top women's college, and her reputation as a posh socialite did little to endear her to her new intellectual classmates. Once again she got straight As but made no real friends. She dated men but never discussed her relationships and her boyfriends knew that the relationship would not go far. Her father wrote her letters, telling her not to give in to men's advances, but Jackie didn't seem to need his advice.

In the summer of 1948 she went abroad for the first time. Every minute of her seven-week tour of Europe's cultural centers had been prearranged. She and her three girlfriends and their chaperone were admitted to a garden party at Buckingham Palace, where Jackie shook hands with Winston Churchill. The group then journeyed on through France, Switzerland, and Italy. Jackie thought that Europe was the height of sophistication and longed to go back as soon as possible. Her father couldn't understand her passion, while her mother spent her time setting up the perfect home— now with twenty-five permanent staff.

In August 1949 Jackie went to France on a Junior Year Abroad program. After a short course at the University of Grenoble, she went to the Sorbonne, living with a French family in Paris. Despite the relative modesty of her surroundings, Jackie always described this as the high point of her life. By the time she returned to the States she no longer wished to attend an all-girls college and had her credits transferred to the more liberal George Washington University. She also entered a *Vogue* writing competition and, of the 1,280 students who applied, Jackie came out on top. She was flown to New York to have her photograph taken by Horst P. Horst and to be introduced to *Vogue*'s editors. The prize was a student traineeship at the magazine,

The Life and Times of

but Janet and Hugh thought that this was a vulgar position and wouldn't let Jackie accept it. As recompense they agreed to pay for her and her sister, Lee, to spend the summer of 1951 in Europe—a trip that was also to serve as a graduation present for both girls, Jackie having got her bachelor's degree from George Washington University and Lee having graduated from Miss Porter's. The two girls had a wonderful time, learning about art in Venice and Florence and staying with local aristocrats.

Jackie Onasssis

CAREER?

Returning to the United States was an anticlimax. Jackie didn't know what to do with herself and she asked Hugh if he might find her something in Washington. Hugh telephoned his friend Arthur Krock, the Washington correspondent of the *New York Times*, who in turn telephoned his friend Frank Waldrop, the editor of a local newspaper called the *Washington Times-Herald*. The *Times-Herald* was the least important paper in the capital and Waldrop wasn't too bothered either way. Jackie said that she would start work after Christmas but in December she met a man named John Husted, and within weeks the couple were engaged. Though they barely knew each other, the wedding was apparently set for June.

Jackie rather vaguely began working at the paper anyway, and though no one took her seriously she was given the featherweight post of "Inquiring Photographer." She had to roam the streets with a camera and then interview passers-by about "questions of the week." Some of her chosen topics included "Should playboys get married?" and "Would you like to crash high society?" Her main problem was that she didn't know how to take a photograph but her secondary one was that everyone in the office thought that she was a socialite who would soon leave to get married. They regarded her with lighthearted tolerance and mocked her for refusing to go out in the rain. Though the men in the office appreciated her good looks, they didn't actually want to help her, and her female colleagues considered her to be flighty and from a different social set. Jackie soon became fed up with first her job and then with her fiancé. At Merrywood, Hugh's Virginia estate, she threw parties whose guests comprised men and women in their fifties and sixties. She had few friends of her own age.

One of her admirers was a married man named Charles Bartlett, whose wife astutely invited Jackie to a small dinner party at which she seated her guest next to a dashing young politician from Boston. He was John F. Kennedy. Jackie had met him at a similar dinner party the Bartletts had given a year before, but at that time nothing had come of the Bartletts' attempts to throw the two together. This time, however, Jack, as he was known, invited Jackie out on a date. Though he was busy campaigning to be elected senator from Massachussets, he called Jackie whenever he was in town and the couple would go to the movies or out for dinner. After several months Jackie knew exactly what she wanted from life. Out of the blue she called John Husted, to whom she was still engaged, and invited him to visit for the weekend. They spent a pleasant enough weekend together; on Sunday evening she drove him to the airport and, as they entered the terminal building, Jackie slipped off her engagement ring and dropped it into his pocket. The pair never saw each other again.

JFK was a whole different ballgame. He had a reputation as a cold, ruthless operator. Although Jackie knew this, she was primarily attracted to the idea of a man of potential power who might one day be at the center of important events. By November 1952 JFK had been elected as Democratic senator from Massachusetts. Along with his good looks, charm, and money, it was clear that he was frighteningly ambitious. He was also Catholic, just like Jackie. Jackie's campaign to win his hand in marriage was plotted down to the last detail. When she learned that he brought a packed lunch to work, she began dropping in at his office with a more tempting lunch—for two. Eventually she helped him write several speeches, and she composed a term paper for his brother, Teddy, then an undergraduate at Harvard. She ran Jack's errands for him and she took him shopping and bought him a whole new wardrobe.

In the summer of 1952 Jackie had spent several days at the Kennedy compound in Hyannis Port, Cape Cod, where she met Rose Kennedy, Jack's mother, and his formidable father, Joe, who had made millions. The whole compound was a frenzy of activity. Jackie flirted with Joe and constantly dropped hints about her (fake) aristocratic French background. Joe became a hearty supporter of this elegant and sophisticated woman and he thought that Jackie would endow Jack's campaign with a bit of class. Joe ordered his son to propose.

The Kennedys' wedding

WEDDING OF THE YEAR

By mid-May 1953 the deed was done, but the engagement announcement had to wait since the *Saturday Evening Post* was currently running a story about "Jack Kennedy—the ultimate bachelor" and JFK didn't want to ruin the effect. On the first permissible day, June 24, 1953, Jacqueline Bouvier handed in her resignation at the *Times-Herald* and her engagement was announced to the press. Jackie arrived at the Kennedy home just a few days later, to be greeted by the harsh realities of her new life. The beautiful young bride was introduced to a *Life* magazine photographer and told that he would spend the next three days following her and Jack around and taking photos of their every move. Jackie was unenthusiastic but Jack's domineering sisters told her it was her duty.

The wedding plans, too, became the subject of dispute. Janet and Jackie wanted a private affair. Joe Kennedy wanted a media circus. The Kennedys won. In September they held a prewedding bash for over 350 important politicians in Boston and then they turned Hyannis Port into a virtual amusement park for over a week. Parties were thrown, including a stag night for Jack hosted by Hugh Auchincloss. Black Jack, staying at a nearby hotel, was excluded from every family event.

The big day—September 12, 1953—finally came. Jackie had insisted that her father give her away but, when his brothers-in-law went to pick him up that morning, they found him lying on the floor, blind drunk. Not knowing what to do they telephoned Janet, who told them to ignore him— her second husband would walk his stepdaughter down the aisle instead. Over three thousand spectators crowded around St. Mary's in Newport, Rhode Island, to see the thirty-six-year-old local hero marry his gorgeous twenty-four-year-old bride. There were 750 guests; the service was conducted by the Archbishop of Boston, and Bobby Kennedy was best man. The reception was held at Hugh's Hammersmith Farm and Jackie, though terribly upset about her father's absence, maintained perfect composure for the two and a half hours it took to shake the hands of all her guests. That evening the couple took a private jet to the Waldorf-Astoria in New York and then flew on to Acapulco, Mexico, where the country's president, an associate of Joe Kennedy's, had lent them one of his private villas. Jackie's first act was to write a letter to her father. Her second was to write to Rose Kennedy. In neither letter did she mention Jack's habit of flirting with every woman they came across, just days after their wedding.

On holiday in Ireland, 1967

Jackie with her children

MARRIED LIFE

On their return from the honeymoon, the Kennedys, who didn't have a house of their own, divided their time between the various family estates and spent that Christmas with Jack's parents. The tone was set for Jackie when she gave her husband an expensive oil painting kit and, without asking permission, his sisters immediately set upon it and helped themselves to all the oils. Jackie was furious but the Kennedys didn't notice. They had no concept of money; their family estate was valued at about $500 million. Joe Kennedy, who had once been U.S. Ambassador to Great Britain, had amassed a fortune on the financial marketplace and now spent all of his money on furthering his political ambitions through his sons. Both he and Rose were notoriously penny-pinching and their servants constantly left because of low pay.

Jackie also had to face up to the propensities of the Kennedy men—about which she had been warned. All had had numerous affairs, generally sharing their girlfriends in a free-for-all arrangement. Joe had had a three-year affair with the film star Gloria Swanson, often conducted in hotel rooms adjacent to his wife. For Joe, no woman was off limits. Rose was a devout Catholic and left him to it. Jackie, probably because of her own father, admired Joe but came to regard Rose with contempt.

By the summer of 1954 Jack was already asking his staff to

organize "house parties" as a regular event. Jackie apparently never mentioned them, though she can hardly have failed to be aware that Jack was in constant competition with his father and his brothers to see who could sleep with the most women.

Despite her early ambition never to be a housewife, Jackie now did little else. She tried to learn about cooking and she helped Jack with his clothes and his speeches. When Jack went into the hospital in New York for critical back surgery in October 1954, Jackie took over many of his duties while Jack spent months in bed recuperating and writing a book about eight important political figures. Called *Profiles in Courage,* it was published in 1956 to rave reviews and went straight into the best-seller lists, later winning the Pulitzer Prize for biography. It is now generally accepted that much of the book was in fact written by a number of academics, including Jackie's former professor of American history.

A party in mid-June 1955 marked Jack's return to the political arena. Jackie thought that most politicians were boring and that their wives were a little dull. She didn't attend every function and Jack was delighted since it gave him the opportunity to rent a permanent apartment in the Mayflower Hotel in Washington, D.C., to which he went regularly with a variety of young women. Fortuitously for Jack his sister Pat married film star Peter Lawford at this time, and Peter's friend Frank Sinatra was a constant source of new telephone numbers and dates. Guests at the Mayflower during this fruitful period included Audrey Hepburn, Betty Grable, Judy Garland, and Marlene Dietrich. Jackie (who had had a miscarriage the previous year) was now seven months' pregnant, but this didn't stop Jack from taking a young starlet as his companion on a trip to Hollywood. Jackie remained, as ever, inscrutable.

In August Jack came within thirty votes of being elected vice president of the Democratic party, and the Kennedys realized that this meant there were now no limits on Catholics holding positions of power. Their ambitions were growing fast. Jack and Teddy went on vacation to the South of France, where JFK

ELECTION DAYS

It was Joe Kennedy's campaign. He enlisted the help of Frank Sinatra and the whole entertainment circus came along for the ride. Joe was the first person to realize the value of political polls and subsequently targeted public-relations exercises. He made all the Kennedy ladies give fund-raising teas and the campaign became the most highly subsidized ever to have taken place. He told Jackie to speak Spanish in New York, French in New Orleans, and Polish in Milwaukee and encouraged her to appear on television regularly and to criss-cross the country scores of times in a private plane bought for the occasion. She shook hands with hundreds of people every day. After the dowdiness of Eleanor Roosevelt and Mamie Eisenhower, the American people were thrilled. Jackie was glamorous, regal, unapproachable; together Jack and Jackie were the American dream.

In July 1960 JFK became the Democratic party leader and he chose Lyndon Johnson as his prospective vice president. Jackie told friends that she hadn't even read the party manifesto. Sitting five seats away from her husband in New York, she joked that this was the nearest she had gotten to him in months. November heralded the first-ever televised election debates—with personal appearance becoming increasingly important in the political arena, Jack met Richard Nixon head on. Election day was November 8, 1960, and by 7 A.M.

the next morning, Jack knew that he was the youngest president-elect in the history of the United States, though he had a majority of less than 115,000 votes out of a total of nearly 70 million. Overnight his life had changed. The Kennedy compound, where the family had gathered to await the results, was immediately surrounded by security police and everyone inside, including Janet and Hugh, immediately started calling him "Mr. President."

Just a few weeks later Jackie gave birth to John, Jr., who was tiny and slightly premature but healthy. As soon as she felt better, Jackie began the serious business of being the First Lady. She went on a search for a new fashion designer. On January 19, 1961, preliminary to the inauguration, the Kennedys attended a reception at which ten thousand guests paid $1,000 each to hear Ella Fitzgerald, Harry Belafonte, and Frank Sinatra sing. At the actual inauguration the next day, Jackie watched poet Robert Frost read one of his poems (her own idea) and then heard her husband sworn in as the thirty-fifth president of the United States. They went to lunch at the White House while family members went to a reception at the Mayflower Hotel and the whole clan met up later for a ball at the White House. Pleading fatigue, Jackie stayed in bed. Her mother had to drag her downstairs and Jackie, looking gorgeous, eventually managed three of the five balls arranged for the evening. Jack managed all five, plus a private one arranged by Peter Lawford. By the morning he looked tired but fully satisfied.

Jackie with her son, 1979

State visit of Pandit Nehru and Indira Ghandi

LIFE IN THE WHITE HOUSE

Jackie soon began the laborious task of setting up home in the White House with its eighteen bedrooms on her floor alone. Within the first month she had already exhausted the $50,000 allocated by the White House budget for the renovation of the family's quarters but she politely pointed out that the apartments had been set up for an elderly couple (the Eisenhowers) and were totally unsuitable for her young family. She was immediately allocated more money.

Shrugging off responsibility for the more traditional First Lady roles, she sent Lady Bird Johnson, the vice president's wife, to over fifty official charity functions in her place in the first year. Instead of attending these events, she spent her time inaugurating new cultural evenings and reorganizing the White House. She invited luminaries like Margot Fonteyn to dance for the president, and she demanded walls of solid shrubs in the grounds so that stray photographers couldn't take snapshots of her children playing on the lawns. Her hatred of all journalists grew even more intense and she now had the Secret Service agents to deal with also. Jackie's own agent followed her everywhere and, much to her annoyance, waited outside while she went to the bathroom.

Her husband's agents, meanwhile, thought that they'd landed the best job in the universe. The president's life was a twenty-four-hour party zone and, though there was an unending stream of women and wine, not one of them sold their story to the press—the lifestyle was too enjoyable to give up for mere financial reward. Wherever he went, advance agents set up dates ahead of his arrival and, back at the White House, his Secret Service agent remained in constant communication with Jackie's agent so that her husband would be informed of her precise arrival home. The White House private pool parties during Jackie's absence became legendary.

In the early summer of 1961 the Kennedys went on a public-relations trip to Paris and it turned into a personal triumph for Jackie. JFK began his official speech with the words "I do not think it entirely inappropriate to introduce myself . . . I am the man who accompanied Jacqueline Kennedy to Paris." Her fashions and hairstyle were the talk of the town. General de Gaulle described her as "charming and ravishing" and is also said to have remarked after their departure that he could see Jackie in about ten years "on the yacht of a Greek oil millionaire." The couple flew on to Vienna, where the president met Soviet Premier Nikita Khruschev, and then on to London to be greeted by Prime Minister Harold Macmillan and a cheering crowd. In London they attended a banquet at Buckingham Palace.

Back in Washington Jackie designed a grand plan to revitalize the White House and its surrounding area. Her children now went to a kindergarten she had set up in the White House. She personally sorted through twenty-six thousand items, selecting the valuable and disposing of the worthless. She appointed a permanent curator to catalogue her findings and she prepared the very first guidebook to the White House. She also recorded an hour-long televised tour of the White House that was broadcast on Valentine's Day 1962 and watched by forty-six million people. On one occasion Martin Luther King, Jr., came to the building to discuss the current race riots when his elevator was suddenly diverted and went shooting down to the basement. An uncharacteristically messy Jackie got in to

The Life and Times of

the elevator and greeted him with the words "Oh, Dr. King, you would be so thrilled . . . I have just discovered a . . . wonderful, beautiful chair," and, arriving at the president's floor, Jackie rushed out ahead of Martin Luther King, saying that she just had to tell Jack about the chair.

At the end of 1961 Joe Kennedy had a stroke. Always fond of him, Jackie was perhaps the only person not to find the drooling old man repulsive. Jack, formerly dependent on his father for advice, now began to lean more and more on his brother Bobby and on Jackie for support.

It was Jackie who spoke to the Bay of Pigs veterans in Spanish after they returned dispirited to Miami. On March 8, 1962, Jackie, taking Lee with her, left the U.S. for a private audience with Pope John XXIII. She flew on to India for a private audience with Prime Minister Nehru and was showered with gifts while the international press criticized her for wearing high fashion in a country riddled with poverty. By the time she stopped in London on her way home, she had become a major world celebrity and enjoyed a private lunch with Queen Elizabeth. This high profile came at a price, though: Jackie's clothing bill for three months during this period came to $35,000, and her personal expenditure for 1962 totaled $121,461.

On May 19 large numbers of celebrities attended a gala in honor of JFK's birthday (on May 29) at Madison Square Garden in New York. The show—organized by Frank Sinatra—was stolen by Marilyn Monroe singing "Happy Birthday, Mr. President." Marilyn was to die of a drug overdose just three months later.

By April 1963 Jackie was once again pregnant. Public interest in her continued to increase and the White House press office, with its five employees, fielded hundreds of questions a day—most of which were about Jackie's shoe size. Jackie, suffering a painful pregnancy, did not accompany the president on his famous trip to Berlin in June. In August she gave birth to a premature son who died after just three days.

Jackie's sister, Lee, had become friendly with Greek shipping tycoon Aristotle Onassis, who invited the two sisters for a recuperative vacation on his yacht *Christina*. Jackie accepted. Jack and Bobby were not amused. Ari was a jet-setting foreigner with a rather dubious reputation and several legal battles with the U.S. tax office behind him. Jack insisted that Stas Radziwill, and the Undersecretary of Commerce, Franklin D. Roosevelt, Jr., and his wife accompany the two women.

The *Christina* was sumptuous and massive. Ari had had it decked out with gladiola, roses, and a sixty-piece orchestra. He was all charm and assiduousness. Jackie and Lee had a marvelous time but soon Jackie had to return to the States to help JFK with the beginnings of his reelection campaign. He was planning a trip to Texas and wanted to be seen with his loving wife. On November 22, 1963, the couple was in Fort Worth; the next morning, their plane touched down in Dallas for a big testimonial. The cavalcade left the airport at 12:55 and was headed up by the president and Jackie in an open-top Lincoln, also carrying Texas governor John Connally and his wife. At precisely 1:30 the car passed the Texas School Book Depository. From a sixth-floor window, an assassin presumed to be a low-life criminal named Lee Harvey Oswald aimed his gun at the president and fired. The first shot hit Jack in the back of the neck; a second severely wounded Governor Connally; a third struck the president and blew away a quarter of his skull. Within six minutes the Lincoln had arrived at Parkland Memorial Hospital but there was nothing that the doctors could do. Jack had been killed instantly.

Jackie's clothes were so bloodstained on arrival at the hospital that the doctors thought that she too had been shot. She refused sedatives and clung to her husband's hand while the official announcement of his death was broadcast at 2:31. Vice President Lyndon Johnson, who had been at the back of the motorcade, arrived at the hospital to take over

The Life and Times of

the reigns of power. He ordered the casket to be carried to Air Force One and, with the plane waiting on the tarmac, Johnson had himself sworn in as president. Jackie stood by in tears and then returned to the plane. Air Force One took off for Washington and everyone on the plane sat, silently, in a state of total shock.

At the Washington airport, Bobby climbed on board and saw Jackie with her husband's blood still splattered on her clothes. Johnson headed straight for the White House and Jackie, still in a state of shock, followed. Just a few days later she heard that Oswald, in turn, had been shot dead by Jack Ruby; her only comment was "one more awful thing," after which she changed the subject—she would later dismiss suggestions that Jack's assassination should be more deeply investigated by changing the subject. Days later millions of people watched as Jackie, with a child in each hand, left the White House and accompanied the coffin to the Capitol Rotunda, where she waited for the first of 250,000 mourners to file by.

Jackie and Bobby began arranging a suitable funeral at Arlington National Cemetery. The guests would include twenty representatives from 102 nations and eleven heads of government, including Britain's Prince Philip and France's Charles de Gaulle. Jackie gave one major interview, to a journalist from *Life* magazine. She told him that the musical *Camelot* was Jack's favorite record and requested that the journalist use this as a metaphor for her dead husband's life. After the article appeared the whole Kennedy administration became known as Camelot—a magical time during which all things seemed possible.

Jackie and Aristotle Onassis

POSTFUNERAL YEARS

Jackie finally left the White House on December 6. The Johnsons, realizing that Jackie was a valuable public-relations asset, gave her a private office in the building and encouraged her to appear there as often as possible, but she always refused to go back. She spent her days with Bobby and the children, and her new house became Washington's number one tourist attraction. In January she went on television to thank the American people for their condolences. She had now become a folk heroine and was virtually a prisoner in her own home.

In February 1964 she made a short trip to New York and realized that the only way to start a new life would be to move out of Washington and start again in Manhattan. She bought a fifteen-room apartment on Fifth Avenue and spent $124,000 on redecoration. Her sister now lived just down the street and Bobby Kennedy was soon to move to the city; speculations grew about Jackie's relationship with him. By January 1965 Jackie began to feel a little better and started to go out again in public, though she was intensely paranoid about any real or imagined invasion of her privacy. She had less and less to do with her old Washington acquaintances and preferred not to have her memories raked up. She divided her weekdays between the gym and artistic foundations, spent her weekends in

New Jersey riding horses, and went on vacation to exotic places.

In November 1967, accompanied by the recently widowed Lord Harlech (giving rise to rumors of a prospective marriage), she undertook a semi-political mission to Cambodia to meet Prince Sihanouk and to try to stem the flow of anti-American feeling in the country. In March 1968 Bobby, who continued to see the Kennedy children almost every day, became a senator for New York, the first step in his path to the presidency. He heard reports that Jackie had continued to see Aristotle Onassis since her recuperative cruise on his boat; although this seemed unlikely, he asked her if the rumors of her impending marriage to the Greek were true. Jackie, as ever, was less than open, but that Easter she flew to Palm Beach with Onassis and her children.

On June 6, 1968, Bobby was shot and died just a few minutes after his victory in the crucial California primary. If it hadn't been before, Jackie's mind was now made up for good. "I hate this country," she said, "I despise America and I don't want my children to live here. If they're killing Kennedys, my kids are number one targets." Onassis was at least sixty-two and Jackie was thirty-nine but the marriage was more or less sealed the day that Bobby died. She flew to Greece with Teddy Kennedy to meet Ari's children, Christina and Alex, though neither of them warmed to Jackie. Teddy informed Ari that, were she to remarry, Jackie would no longer get trust money from the Kennedys; and, of course, neither would she get her widow's pension. Ari wasn't bothered—he was infinitely wealthier than all the Kennedys combined. He agreed to give Jackie $3 million dollars as a kind of reverse dowry and $1 million for each of her children. In his office Jackie became known as "supertanker" since buying her had cost their boss more than most of his fleet.

On October 15, 1968, the news—up to then a secret— was announced in the press and Jackie decided that the wedding now had to take place immediately. Ari happened to own Olympic airways, and that day ninety regular passengers were "bounced" from a scheduled flight to Greece so that Jackie and her entourage could have their seats. They met Ari there and, pursued by some three hundred reporters, flew on to Skorpios, Ari's private island. At first Ari's own children refused to attend, but after much cajoling they witnessed the ceremony, on October 20, while Jackie's own children stood by quietly.

Aristotle Onassis

ONASSIS YEARS

"Jackie Weds Blank Cheque" announced London's *Daily Mirror*. "America Has Lost a Saint" said Germany's *Bild Zeitung*. "This Woman Now Lives in a State of Spiritual Degradation" observed the Vatican's *L'Osservatore della Domenica*. No one could believe that the world's fairy-tale heroine had voluntarily chosen to marry an antique toad: she *must* have done it for the money. The public simply couldn't accept that their saint had sunk so low. By October 24 Ari had already flown away on business and Caroline and John Jr. had returned to school in New York. Jackie was left alone on Skorpios. Many of Onassis's friends considered that he had made a big mistake and that he should have married his soulmate—the adoring Maria Callas—but the first year of his marriage seemed to go well enough. Jackie got an expense account and a $1 million diamond ring for her fortieth birthday, and Ari didn't hold back on his continuing encounters with Callas.

Still, he did make an effort with Jackie's children. He bought John Jr. a speedboat, a jukebox, and a mini-jeep and he went to all of the kids' school plays. Contrarily, Jackie made absolutely no effort with either Christina or Alex and all three remained in a prolonged state of mutual dislike. Ari wanted his daughter, now twenty-three, to marry the son of one of his business colleagues and told Jackie to encourage

Christina to agree. On February 3, 1971, Jackie returned to the White House for the first and last time to unveil the official portraits of herself and JFK at a private dinner given by President and Mrs. Nixon. Back in Greece Christina announced the first of many disastrous marriages (to a forty-eight-year-old businessman) and Ari's first wife, Christina's mother, announced her intention to marry her brother-in-law, her sister having died of a barbiturates overdose.

The disaster bell tolled once more when ten photographers donned diving outfits and took nineteen photos of Jackie nude on a beach. These first appeared in an Italian version of *Playboy* and subsequently in other magazines and papers, including American ones. Onassis, who thought it was funny, refused to give Jackie the money to sue. She, in turn, prevented him from staying in her Fifth Avenue apartment in New York; meanwhile he began to be irritated by her overexpenditure: her bills now came to around $50,000 a month.

Stories of Jackie's propensity for spending only other people's money abounded. Some Iranian friends of hers invited her and Ari to stay at their hotel in Teheran for a week and the couple ran up a bill of $650,000. Although the entire bill was to be picked up by their hosts, nonetheless Jackie's secretary required them to pay for their airfare on Olympic— and in advance. When a carpenter arrived to build some shelves, Jackie offered him an autographed photo rather than a check. Other workmen were offered her personal endorsement in lieu of fees. At the same time, she was a compulsive shopper. Ari saw Maria Callas more and more frequently and Jackie told her friends that he was vulgar. By the end of 1971 the couple barely spoke.

On January 22, 1973, soon after his twenty-fourth birthday, Alex Onassis, Ari's son and heir, died in a plane crash. Ari was devastated. He knew that Alex had hated Jackie and felt that he hadn't done enough to support his son against his new wife. He also felt that Jackie didn't share his grief and he soon became ill and depressed and then rewrote his will, leaving virtually everything to Christina. To add insult to injury he made Athina, his first wife, the chief executor of his will. She, however, died of a drug overdose not long after. Christina and all the rest of the Onassis family felt that Jackie was a curse and they pleaded with Ari to get a divorce as quickly as possible. Ari didn't want Jackie to know about his plans since he thought this would be tactically disastrous. His fears seemed well founded since, although he was now extremely ill, his wife seemed to spend most of his money traveling away from him.

Early in February 1975 Ari collapsed with chest pains and was rushed to the hospital in Paris. Christina and Jackie both spent every day at the hospital, though Christina would leave the room as soon as Jackie arrived and Jackie spent every evening at fancy restaurants with friends. After a few weeks Jackie returned to the United States for a skiing vacation. She was still in New York when Onassis died of bronchial pneumonia on March 15. The funeral took place in Skorpios and was followed by a bitter eighteen-month legal dispute between Jackie and Christina over his $1 billion estate. Jackie's lawyers eventually settled for a mere $20 million, which meant that her total income from Ari came to $42 million, or nearly $7 million for each year of their married life. Christina's balance, however, brought her little comfort since she soon grew addicted to drugs and married and divorced four times, lastly to Thierry Roussel, by whom she had a daughter named Athina. After Christina's death in 1988 Athina went to live with her father and his new wife in Switzerland; she is the world's wealthiest young teenager. Jackie did not attend Christina's funeral.

With Maurice Tempelsman

LATER YEARS

Jackie, meanwhile, returned to New York, where she learned to paint in watercolor and began to look for a new role in life. In September 1975 it was announced that Jackie was going to start work as a consulting editor at Viking Press at a salary of $10,000 a year. She commissioned coffee table books and did little actual editing, but it was a public-relations coup for the firm to have her on their premises. In 1977 Jackie resigned from the company and was immediately offered a new, higher-profile post at Doubleday. She worked three days a week; here, too, her primary function was as a publicity vehicle for the firm. Jackie didn't socialize with the people at work, but did date a few men in the evenings, though most of these were discouraged by the constant press attention. They were inevitably followed by photographers and asked questions about their intentions. If they ever took her to dinner with friends, everyone in the room simply fell silent at the star witness to the glorious years of the American Dream.

Jackie was now fifty. She bought herself an estate on Martha's Vineyard, the most exclusive island in the exclusive Cape Cod region. She had a house designed for her; by the time it was finished in 1981 her most frequent houseguest was her former financial adviser, Maurice Tempelsman. Tempelsman and his wife, Lily, had first met Jackie in the

1950s and were frequent guests at the White House during the Kennedy years. By 1982 Lily, a marriage guidance counselor, had seen so many pictures of her husband of thirty years holding hands with Jackie Onassis that she asked him to vacate the matrimonial home.

Jackie now cast off some of her jet-setting, credit-card-holding image and lived fairly quietly with Maurice. In 1983 she had her first major publishing coup when, now promoted to full editor, she personally persuaded Michael Jackson to write his "autobiography" for Doubleday. *Moonwalk* entered the best-seller lists and Jackie was rewarded with a raise.

Jackie's children, meanwhile, were growing up. In 1986 twenty-eight-year old Caroline married forty-one-year-old Edwin Schlossberg, who, like Tempelsman, came from an orthodox Jewish family. At Caroline's Catholic wedding there were 425 guests, twenty-one of whom were friends of Ed. In 1988 Caroline graduated from Columbia Law School and gave birth to Jackie's first grandchild, a girl they named Rose. Caroline had two more children, in 1990 and 1993, and Jackie reveled in her role as grandmother.

Another 1986 wedding saw Caroline's cousin Maria Shriver marry film star Arnold Schwarzenegger. In 1988 Jackie's sister married film director Herbert Ross, and one of the guests at that wedding was film star Daryl Hannah. John Jr. met her at the reception and the pair started dating; he also began working at the Manhattan office of a District Attorney, having finally managed to pass the New York Bar Exam on his third attempt.

By the late '80s Maurice Tempelsman and Jackie were inseparable, though he was still not legally divorced. After Bill Clinton was elected president in 1992, Hillary Clinton became the only First Lady whom Jackie had ever invited to visit her at home. The Clintons were delighted by this public-relations coup and later joined Jackie and Maurice for an afternoon on Maurice's yacht. In 1993 John Jr. gave up working as a lawyer and rumors of his impending marriage to

Daryl Hannah and his mother's general disapproval hit the papers. But that relationship eventually ended and in September 1996, in a secret ceremony, John Jr. married longtime girlfriend Caroline Bessette. He also founded a political magazine called *George*.

In December 1993 Jackie developed a swelling in the groin that was diagnosed as cancer of the lymph system. Her son moved into a local hotel and her daughter visited daily. She gave up her lifetime habit of chain smoking but, by mid-March, the situation was hopeless. Tempelsman rarely left her side. With no cure possible, she asked to be allowed to spend her remaining days in peace at home. Jackie Bouvier Kennedy Onassis died on May 19, 1994, at sixty-four years of age. Her funeral took place on May 23 in New York, after which her body was flown to Arlington National Cemetery so she could join her first husband. Bill and Hillary Clinton stood behind in reverential silence while John Jr. and Caroline kissed their mother's coffin and said good-bye to a legend forever.

INDEX